BREAKING THE CHAINS

of Pastoral Bondage

Navigating to Leadership
Freedom

BISHOP MICHAEL FULLER

Revised Version

Breaking the Chains of Pastoral Bondage
Copy Right © 2013 Bishop Michael Fuller
Revised Edition © 2017
Breaking the Chains of Pastoral Bondage: Navigating to Leadership
Freedom
ISBN-13: 978-0-9995227-0-7
ISBN-10: 0-9995227-0-7
NJ Publishing Fayetteville, NC
Book Cover design: MRF Graphics & Music © 2013 © 2017

Table of Contents

Foreword

Greetings in the name of our Lord, Jesus Christ:

The current crisis and bondage of pastors and leaders in need of deliverance, healing, and restoration to their God given potential, caused me to write this book. The pastors and leaders of this generation are crying out for help and restoration.

This book centers upon principles of leadership that are critical to the well-being and spiritual health of the pastor and leaders alike. There are various challenges that have crippled the men and women of God when it comes to serving the people. Knowing how far to go in the process of leading and being able to maintain spiritual stability are a few things that I will touch basis on here in this book.

Too many times the enemy has caused great leaders to succumb to mental and emotional attacks which leave them bound in a chain of bondages.

Most of us find that the experiences of ministry do not always have a pleasant outcome. It can push you to the very brink of leaving the ministry because of the rash of discouragements that can continually come your way.

I encourage each pastor and leader to embrace this book. This will change your life and perspective about ministry. It is my prayer that every pastor and leader in the body of Christ be victorious in your pursuit to carry out your Kingdom assignment and to remain healthy and vibrant in your faith. We must stand together in prayer and take back what the enemy has stolen from us.

Bishop M. Fuller

Can There Really be Bondages in the Life of a Pastor?

The principles shared in this book are based upon many years of Christian experiences that have been lived out in my life. People have many times misunderstood the calling in the pulpit to mean something glamorous and prestigious when in reality it can be one of the loneliest places one could ever experience.

When I came into ministry in the early 1980's the church was a place of great honor and respect for the pastor or leaders. People would reach out in ways to ensure that the man of God was recognized as the spiritual leader, but something happened over time to infiltrate the office that God had established in the earth. He said that:

"He would give us pastors after His own heart that would feed the people with knowledge and understanding." (Jeremiah 3:15)

Over the course of my years in ministry, I saw a great transition in leadership roles, functions, and duties as it relates to the church. The enemy has launched an attack to bind the very ones who were called to bind up his works by operating through the minds of the people in the church. Many leaders suffer from exhaustion and burnout because the enemy launched what I call a "needy spirit" in the church. People began to need the pastor's attention more like a personal nurse than a spiritual leader.

Many pastors run around to any and every event that involves their members to show moral support and to let the member know they don't have to leave the church because you're going to cater to their every beck and call. What seems to be ministry is actually a mental bondage for the pastor. If you don't go they may leave your ministry with the mindset that you didn't care about them or never came to see them. This creates the bondage of separation.

Many pastors or leaders experience separation anxieties from fear of losing members.

The pastor is put in the position to compete for the members loyalty so they pay bills, buy clothes, pick up children, attend social events, funerals, etc., to look in the eye of their members as being a pastor who cares about their well-being. If you accomplish this feat of attending to each member this way, when will you as a pastor have time for prayer, study, planning, renewal, and your own family?

The enemy has accomplished his goal of leading us to think that we're fulfilling our pastoral call by putting us in chains unawares. We're running around and wearing ourselves out, not even realizing that we're locked in a place of bondage.

The early church apostles recognized early in their ministry that they couldn't settle every dispute and meet everyone's need by themselves. There was a dispute about the proper distribution and care for the widows who were of Greek culture verses the Hebrews. The apostles saw this conflict interfering with their true calling and work and stated,

"It is not reason that we should leave the word of God, and serve tables. Wherefore,

brethren, look ye out among you seven men of honest report, full of the Holy Ghost and wisdom, whom we may appoint over this business. But we will give ourselves continually to prayer, and to the ministry of the word." (Acts 6:2-4).

We're not called to lavish people with gifts so they will remain loyal to us an under-shepherd. We have to stay free from emotional and mental bondages that will keep us from operating in our true calling. If we don't grab hold to this concept then the enemy will use the very people assigned to us to put us in bondage and watch us dry up and fade away.

Often times some of the very people you gave out to will not stay with you and it can create an emotional disconnect for you in the long run. You will start feeling unappreciated because of all you did for the people and they still told you off and didn't treat you right as a leader. This may have been a sign that you were trying to buy your members instead of pastor them.

We don't pastor with gifts, but with the Word of God.

When a pastor is in bondage to his/her own members, it creates a dangerous playground for the enemy. Your very anointing can be stifled because of the physical and emotional interference that we have allowed as leaders to blind us to our true purpose. I believe many leaders walk in bondage today, especially if you have a small congregation, to try to compete to see if we can hold on to the ones we have near us by giving them assignments in ministry that they're really not qualified to hold. Again, we put ourselves as leaders in bondage.

We give special privilege and favor so they will remain loyal. We must face the truth and realize that we're in a situation where we have lost our focus on ministry and have started to dictate based upon our numbers. We have to trust what God has called us to do and seek to stay in His will.

I remember many days early on in ministry experiencing anxiety, headaches, and stress because I was engrossed on making things happens for the ministry. I would try to visit each member, call through the week to check up on them, provide counseling, and help in other ways as necessary. I found myself in bondage to my own vision. I would abandon my own family for the sake of going to see about someone else's family. Not only can we put ourselves personally in bondage, but our entire household will begin to decay and suffer.

Now, the enemy has accomplished two things: one he caused the leader to serve blindly and wear out his/her spiritual strength, and secondly, an open door of family neglect was created which gave the enemy entrance to create division amongst the leader's family.

This creates a vacuum where now the enemy works behind the scene to bring disturbance and disruption to the leaders' household to create an even greater bondage. All of sudden, the pastor is chained by his/her own circumstance and rendered ineffective. If we don't come to terms with people, we will end up divorced, separated, backslidden, or just totally out of ministry period. Simply because we failed to recognize that home has to be just as important as the people you serve.

Don't allow your house to be captured by the enemy and put in bondage while you're attentively engaged in freeing someone else's house. Pastoring can be at times a game of cat and mouse. People will play on your emotions, if you let them. They will sometimes try to threaten your ministry and create bondages by refusing to support the vision. They may purposely not give or stay home.

When you try to give them a call out of concern, they may have short conversation with you or will not return your call. Don't allow this tactic to cause you mental anguish and start second guessing your leadership as a pastor. If you play into the mind trap of the enemy, who intentionally distracts you away from his destructive purpose, will find yourself losing sleep and not enjoying your assignment.

The enemy loves to see the pastor suffer and not fulfill his/her kingdom responsibility.

How Do We Get Over the Mess We Created?

When there is a situation concerning pastors or leaders, we typically want to point out the member's role in the mess and eliminate ourselves. In this case, we have to come to the forefront of responsibility and take the lead and the blame for how things may have turned out. We are the pastors so the bondage and situations being experienced must be examined not just from the perspective of the people, but from the upper echelon of leadership.

To repair the breaches that we recognize in our ministry, we have to be willing to say I'm sorry or please forgive me. We may feel that the people are at fault so they should come and repent to the leader, but contrariwise, the leader needs to come before the people. We carry what the people follow and that is the anointing of God.

If we don't show them by example how to handle a situation, they will be content to linger wondering what you as the pastor are going to do about this mess. What created the mess in the first place? We have to ask ourselves as pastors. Did I leave God out of my ministry? Did I put the people before God? Did I make this my ministry instead of the Lord's ministry? Did I neglect my own house and family? Did I assume that the Lord was with me? Did I take on more than I could handle? If you evaluate these questions, you may find that many assumptions that are made about ministry were not God mandates but zeal initiatives.

I think about Joshua when God led him to conquer the city of Ai. Everyone was feeling good about the victory God had just given them. When Israel came upon the bigger City of Jericho, Joshua and the people were so confident in this campaign that they didn't even send out all the soldiers to fight. They thought that God was with them until they were utterly defeated. What was the valuable lesson learned by Joshua who was the leader of the people?

Just because you won one battle doesn't mean that God will be with you in the next one.

We have to check with the Lord first before we engage the ministry to ensure that the Lord is with us. If not, we could experience a big mess that could cause the people to turn against us. This will surely create a bondage. Distrust by the people who say they are with you can cripple some leaders reasoning to keep going when he or she is not fully equipped. What Joshua learned from his experience is that he didn't have time to be sorrowful because the Lord had revealed the problem, and let him know he had to get up and straighten out the mess.

To repair the disappointment and fix the problem, we have to go to God and seek forgiveness. At the same time, we must receive his instructions, recover ourselves, and correct the problem. We must prevent the mess from contaminating the entire body.

After Joshua and Israel lost the battle against the city of Ai, the Lord gave revelation to Joshua why Israel was defeated in the battle. Joshua was so confident that they would win the battle that he didn't consult the

Lord before going into the fight. He was unaware that there was a change in the atmosphere of obedience within the congregation. The disobedience of the people caused sin to enter into the camp. This caused them to fight without the favor of God and suffer defeat.

In order to restore the presence of God to the house, we have to be willing to investigate and find out the root of the problem and deal with it quickly so authority and order can be restored.

If this is not corrected, the people will lose respect for leadership. Joshua's influence over the people would have been hindered.

To keep the enemy from using the people against us, we have to deal with situations as we consult the Lord without favoritism. One of the concepts that the Holy Spirit showed me through Joshua's leadership experience is that we as pastors' have to first cleanup our house before we can move His house. We can cause defeat to the things of God if we don't cleanup our house to ensure everything and everyone is in proper order.

Order causes the house to flow and prosper.

The Apostle Paul stresses this point by saying to Timothy concerning the qualifications of leadership, "For if a man know not how to rule his own house, how shall he take care of the church of God?" *(I Timothy 3: 5)* If we're not good stewards of God's possessions then we will have difficulty providing the appropriate leadership to the church. To break bondages, we must be obedient to God's Word. We must face and resist the enemy's attacks that are sent out to undermine our spiritual authority.

We must know that this is a fight for us concerning the work of the Lord. We can break that defeated tactic by staying before the Lord in prayer, fasting, and studying the Word.

No leader that I know wants to be defeated or seen as weak in the eyes of the people that they serve and lead.

Instead of calling the people in to give an account, you as the leader need to first find out from God where was the breach made. If you find out it was you, then be humbled enough to gather the people and strengthen them with your humble apology. By putting the Lord first, you can rekindle the people's affection and confidence to know that the Lord is with you. Now is not the time to point fingers, but be about the business of getting kingdom matters straighten out so the work of the Lord and can move forward.

You're the point person and must take the lead. What happens next will largely depend upon how you handle yourself and the situation. Don't allow the enemy to cause arrogance to step in and you approach the people out of the wrong spirit. You carry the anointing for the people, so be careful about the name blame and finger pointing. Don't get caught up in the negatives because God is expecting you to clean up the house so that He can continue to bless. Don't ever forget what we always tell others, forgive yourself.

Just because you're the pastor, doesn't mean you will not make a leadership error.

Make sure you learn from the experience and clean up the mess. Also recognize that you do not want to chase members trying to make amends. Call the people together and be honest before them so they can help you clean up the mess. Don't stand back with arms folded like you're beyond human standards and untouchable. Let the people know that you need them as much as they need you. You may feel weighted down for a time because of finding out that you do have to face yourself and recognize that you can fail if not carefully guided by the Lord. Faced with the guilt of having to convince members to remain faithful while you're in your period of recovery can be a difficult challenge.

Every leader is not living in sin, but just when you face certain situations of leadership, it can create some setbacks that we did not have in our vision. Some people may look at you differently because they held you in such high esteem. Don't allow this to become a bondage in your life. Keep moving forward with the vision. Had Joshua stopped because of the defeat at Jericho, he would never have witnessed the awesome presence of God's deliverance to knock down the fortified walls of Jericho in the second campaign by a mere silence and praise. The past defeat taught him how to wait and follow God.

Stop stressing about who is going to follow you on to the promise land. God already has that covered. Just make sure that you keep going and let God determine who is going with you. If you let God give you the people, they will be obedient and follow.

Make sure you don't leave an intact mess and try to move on to the next battle. Get that stuff straight. What will happen if you don't, is that you as a leader, will experience the bondages of the people, the situation, and mess being destroyed. Nothing will be able to stand before you and your God given assignment will not come forth.

I had many days and nights where I struggled to stand against those who were seeking to undermine my calling. There was more discomfort in my spirit and I had many restless nights because God was trying to get my attention concerning the bondages that were manifesting in my life. People had become my focus so much so that I was driven by their actions toward me and the ministry. I stood for what was right, but was always consumed with my decisions to bring discipline when it seemed like we were on our way to the Promised Land. I later came to discover that God was chastening me because I forgot the one command in the Bible that is essential to every believer's spiritual life, which is, *"But seek ye first the kingdom of God, and His righteousness; and all these things shall be added unto you."* *(Matthew 6:33).*

I had allowed the enemy to cause me to count numbers of people and I stopped trusting God. Many times, as pastor's we find ourselves rating the ministry based upon the number of people rather than honoring God and giving Him thanks in all things.

This was a critical mistake because I had opened a door to the enemy to come and cause a mess. I went to the Lord in prayer and He revealed to me and rebuked my lack of faith. He instructed me to never put people in place of Him again. I understood that I wanted God to bless me with people instead of me wanting Him. Putting our confidence in numbers is worldly and fleshly bondage.

We must not make a god out of people.

David made this mistake when the enemy tempted him to number Israel and he got in trouble with God. The Bible says,

"And Satan stood up against Israel, and provoked David to number Israel." *(I Chronicles 21:1)*

When David instructed this of Joab, the Bible says, *"And God was displeased with this thing; therefore, he smote Israel. And David said unto God, I have sinned greatly, because I have done this thing: but now, I beseech thee, do away the iniquity of thy servant; for I have done very foolishly."* *(I Chronicles 21:7-8)*

This is a rare instance in Scripture where we can see God giving one of his leaders one of three choices of punishment after making a mess in I Chronicles 21:9-13. Wow! Thank God for grace and mercy. David told the seer (prophet) that he was in a mess and chose to take God's punishment instead for risking the punishment of man. He said, *"for very great are his mercies: but let me not fall into the hand of man."*

We must be careful not to go against a God given command. Our glory and victory will not rest in numbers, but in the grace and power of God. I found myself at a place where I had to face the Lord's correction for trying to make man match what only God is able to provide. After getting that mess straight with God, I heard the Holy Spirit speak something so profound and prophetic in my spirit that it shook the very foundation of my life.

For the first time in my ministry, I was on the brink of being freed from pastoral bondage. I had gotten my priorities with God so out of order that I almost missed my blessings. Thank God for His rich mercy. He spoke to me in that *"still small voice,"* and gave me four principals in which I was to walk and live by as I carry out His will. These four principals that I am going to share transformed my inner man into a new dimension of faith. Chains of people began to immediately break off my mind and spirit. In one day, my chains of pastoral bondage were completely broken off of my life.

My Bondages Were Broken

It's almost impossible to describe the moment that I had with the Lord. All I know is that when the Lord spoke a *"Rhema"* word into my spirit, *"life"*, I took wings and began to soar to new heights in my ministry.

I was no longer a prisoner of people's opinions or attacks. My headaches, stress level, worrying, and fear of my next meal all dissipated into oblivion. The Lord had set me free from my pastoral bondages. The way I would pastor the Lord's flock would forever be changed in my life. You may be wondering, what was the *"Rhema"* word that the Lord spoke to cause my bondages to be broken.

He spoke four profound statements to me as he was releasing the burdens and bondages off of me:

"Love the Lord thy God with all they heart, mind, and soul, Live Holy, Preach the Gospel & Love the people."

This new revelation from the Lord leap in my Spirit as John the Baptist did as a baby when he *"leaped in his Mother, Elisabeth's womb (Luke 1:41)."*

These four principals were written on the tables of my heart from the Lord. These four Divine principles came from the Lord and encompassed the areas of my ministry assignment: Putting God first, worship and keeping Covenant relationship; Evangelism of the world through the message of Jesus, and discipleship (Seeking to save the lost and making disciples for the kingdom.

I received what I like to call is a *"Redirected Focus."* I was no longer seeking to please the emotions of people because that is what put me in bondage in the first place. Now, it's all about the Kingdom. I had to release what I heard a well-known preacher say in a leadership conference some years ago, *"Give God His wife back!!"*

I stopped committing spiritual adultery by surrendering God's church back to Him. I was in love with the wrong ministry. I was called to *"love God and to keep His commandments."* I had become so emotionally engineered by how the people reacted to my leadership that I began to cater to that in an effort to save face and keep their commitment.

When we allow people to influence our vision then it becomes twisted with human interference which can cause the work to cease. People can attempt to block what God is doing in your life out of shear defiance because they know we depend on them to support our vision. God rebuked my weak use of His strength, and put me back in my place of authority. He reminded me that He was in charge of the people. I had to quickly repent and give God the reigns back over my mind, will, and emotions to keep me from trying to carry a burden that was only meant for God to handle.

Remember when Moses was in the wilderness leading the children of Israel and they continued to murmur and complain about where he was taking them? Moses got to a place where he was fed up. In the Book of Numbers, Chapter 11, Moses had a complaint and spoke a very humbling and profound statement as a leader of Gods people. He said

"I am not able to bear all this people alone, because it is too heavy for me. And if thou deal thus with me, kill me, I pray thee, out of hand, if I have found favor in thy sight; and let me not see my wretchedness." *(verse 14-15)*

What a statement from such an awesome man of God who stood in the very essence of God's glory and still was weighted with bondage. If Moses had to recognize his bondage then how much more should we as leaders today realize that perhaps the enemy has used our very calling against us. I had to release what was weighing me down, "people."

First Principle:

"Love the Lord thy God with all thy heart, and with all thy soul, and with all thy mind." (Matthew 22:37)

The Lord reminded me that he must be my Sovereign Lord in my total being. Everything that I am comes from the Lord.

I began to understand that I had not loved the Lord with all my heart, mind, soul, body, and strength but that I had loved the Lord according to how the people would respond to my leading.

I knew I had *"come short of the glory of God."* Just hearing my Father address my issue and reminding me of where I lacked His grace was a life changer for me. This shook the very foundation of my faith. Sometimes we think that we have everything covered, but when the Lord evaluates us, He informs us of the one thing we still lack. He certainly did this with the rich young ruler who said *"All these things have I kept from my youth up: what lack I yet?" (Matthew 19:20)*

He thought he had it going on and that he kept all the commandments, but Jesus knew his heart was not in the right place. When he was challenged with his worldly goods, he found out that the Lord knew more about his motives than he did. Even so with me; the Lord knew that I had covered a lot of ground but needed a wakeup call so I could break that bondage of feeling like everything was good to go when in reality I was being hindered by my actions that needed correction. I Thank my heavenly Father for loving me enough to chasten me about my love for Him.

Second Principle:
"Live Holy"

I felt like the Prophet Isaiah when He had a vision of the Lord in His glory filling the temple in the book of Isaiah chapter 6. I was again brought to a place of accountability before the Lord. I recognized it was important for me to take back my worship with the Lord. I was so stressed with the daily lives of people that I was trying to play *"Mr. Fix it,"* but I didn't see that I had to maintain my relationship and worship with the Lord.

When we as leaders become so engrossed with helping people in our congregations or community, we must not forget that our character and life must stay in constant communion with the Lord.

We don't just preach to others, we must BE what we preach.

This requires constant worship and communication with the Lord. I thought that helping people I shepherd was a part of living holy. It is to an extent, but, the people should never be our excuse for not staying before the Lord. It's not our job as leaders to try and fix their every problem. If leaders do not stay in the presence of God and seek his guidance, we can step into situations that were not meant for us to be in. We might end up on the short end of the stick because the enemy tricked us to leave our altar to play referee to *"daycare saints."*

The Lord reminded me that I have to live holy by maintaining my relationship with Him. Living Holy requires leaders to stand your ground upon the principles of the Word of God and not on the emotions of the people. My assignment was to show the people how to get to God, but if I have no prayer or worship life then I could hinder not only the people, but myself as well.

I was recharged with a since of urgency to walk with God like never before. If I am going to fulfill my destiny then I must come up a little higher and walk upright before the Lord. The Lord gave Joshua a mandate to walk upright before Him and to observe and keep His law and statutes and to not turn away to the left or the right.

Obedience to Gods instructions insures the favor, blessing, and prosperity of the Lord over our lives. Living a Holy life is worth having the Lord's Grace to break through every barrier and bondage that will try to come against us. I know and accept that living holy is not a choice, but a command.

Third Principle:
"Preach the Gospel"

Can you imagine being a pastor or preacher but not really preaching? I think that this particular principle is amazing. This principal brought me back to the place of my kingdom calling. I was assigned to preach the message of salvation to the people of God. The Lord validated my assignment to the Gospel and that was my pastoral duty. Sometimes we reach out so much physically in an attempt to help people and forget that works doesn't transform them, but that the Word of God certainly will. He wanted me to understand that as an under-shepherd of His flock, I have no other choice but to preach the gospel because it is the word that will set the captives free-not me.

Pastors can come into bondage to preaching when we feel as though we're not reaching the people with the message. We can't overreact to the countenance of the people's faces and allow ourselves to be put in bondage because they look like they're not listening or participating in the delivery of the message.

One religious author wrote a powerful statement by saying to ministers, "the message that I have is not mine." We have to do exactly what Paul told young Timothy, *"I CHARGE, thee therefore before God, and the Lord Jesus Christ, who shall judge the living and the dead at his appearing and his kingdom; Preach the word; be ready in season, out of season; reprove, rebuke, exhort with all long suffering and doctrine."* (2 Timothy 4:1-2)

The Lord never intended for me to preach to keep people because that would put me in bondage to people.

If we don't preach the unaltered and uncompromising truth of the Gospel then we are not really preaching.

I was charged by the Lord to do what I was called to do without fear or rejection or reprisal of the people. In order to set the captives free, we must know as pastors and leaders that we're free to stand on the Word of God even when it may not be popular. I understand even greater that preaching is not a contest to see who can be the most charismatic, or move the emotions of the people. But every pastor has a mandate to glorify God, preach the good news of Jesus

Christ, and reach lost souls who need to be delivered and set free from satanic bondage.

The only way for this to happen is that I, as the Pastor, must not turn away from the dispensation of God that has been committed unto me. We must proclaim the liberty of the Kingdom whether we're popular or not. I have to preach the gospel to hear the Lord Say, *"well done thou good and faithful servant."* Every preacher is not necessarily called by the Lord but I am thankful that my Lord has *"counted me faithful putting me into the ministry."*

Fourth Principle:
"Love the People"

I am thankful for the wisdom of God because He knew the very test of a leader's faith is the very thing that He requires us to do, **LOVE**. I believe one of the worst bondages that a leader can face is having an alt or grudge against the people which he or she leads.

I thank the Lord for reaffirming my responsibility to His commandment to love. The very core of our ministry is truly tied to this principle. When I heard it, I felt that finally I can release my hold on people and stop trying to worry about their every need. All I had to do was love them. I learned through this experience that I loved them, but not enough to trust God to keep them. I also recognized that any disappointments or hurts received from people did not give me reason enough or an excuse not to love them. The Lord was showing me His heart for His Church and that as His under-shepherd, that same love shown would break the bondages and create an environment where they could come and be ministered to without fear or hesitation.

Demonstrating love in spite of the people will put the enemy to a flight and open a new revelation of God's grace in our worship. Love is an igniter of our gifts and by understanding this; I could tap into another dimension of glory that would be released over the house, *"Because the love of God is shed abroad in our hearts by the Holy Ghost which is given unto us."* *(Romans 5:5)*

I soon realized that the Lord was releasing me from something to bring me into something that was far greater than I could imagine. He was waiting for me to come to the place where I needed reviving and a revival in my spirit so He could set me in His love to channel my gifting's and anointing to reach His people at a greater level. *"We know that love covers a multitude of sin."* I am praising the Lord for calling me into His love because it released me to love His people without condition.

When I finally answered the Lord's leading concerning my elevation to the office of Bishop, I didn't realize how these four principles would become so critical in my new capacity as a leader. After my consecration, the Lord gave me an emblem that I call today the seal of the Bishop. When I looked at the finished work of the emblem, I saw that my beginning ministry was bridged along with the new ministry IMFC (International Ministerial Fellowship of Churches) that was being birthed out.

These four principles are wrapped around the outer shield area of the emblem to constantly remind me of my purpose and Covenant, as the servant of the Lord.

Bondages are real and active in the lives of people and especially in pastors and leaders. We can overcome them if we realize the impact that these bondages can have upon our ministry. We can get over the mess we created by having a pure and true acknowledgment of ourselves before God and His people. Transparency brings accountability to both the leader and the people that we lead. Let us not give the enemy another moment to bring blindness or deceit into our hearts and cause us to act innocent to bondages.

We have been anointed to lead the people of God into spiritual freedom and holy living.

Let's begin by doing things God's way and we will see the manifestation of His glory. If we show the people how to break the bondages by using our own lives as godly examples, they will gain strength in their faith to put more effort into their daily walk and truly live out the Christian faith as it was intended.

The Lord is knocking on the door our hearts, and calling us to the forefront of victory. We must stay free so we can effectively carry out this dispensation for which we have been called. Can there really be bondages in the life of a pastor? Yes, there can be many bondages in the life of a pastor.

The enemy understands that if he can *"smite the shepherd, he can scatter the flock."* In light of these truths, every pastor and leader must be renewed and empowered spiritually to *"fight the good fight of faith."* We must break the bondages off our lives so that the people of God can continue to receive from a vessel that understands his or her calling, who has been in battle and who has fought against evil spiritual forces, and knows by faith and experience how to lead the people into victory through Christ.

The Scriptures are filled with historical records of the many great leaders of the faith who had to deal with some type of bondage. Some didn't survive the attack, but many did and were brought back into reality that without the Lord, the enemy could have overtaken them by worldliness.

For an example, look at Abram who deceived Pharaoh and lied that Sarai was his wife or Jacob who stole his brothers birth right to get the blessing. Remember Moses struck the rock when God instructed him to speak to it. We tend to forget about Saul who was the first king of Israel, who got caught up in disobedience and lost his kingdom. David plotted and schemed to kill a man so that he could have his wife. Eli the high priest, got in trouble for not disciplining his two sons for their sinful behavior "in" the church, and one of the greatest tragedy's that we see in the Bible is Samson, who was gifted by God with great strength, but was in bondage to his own desires.

The Scripture in the book of Hebrews says:
"Let us draw near with a true heart in full assurance of faith, having our hearts sprinkled from an evil conscience, and our bodies washed with pure water. Let us hold fast the profession of our faith without wavering; (for he is faithful that promised) And let us consider one another to provoke unto love and to good works." *(Hebrews 10:22-24)*

We can reclaim our dominion and authority through Jesus Christ and live out the true integrity of our calling without bondages. The chains are broken and we're free to serve our Lord. I am praying for every pastor and leader in the Kingdom of our Lord Jesus Christ to come forth in victory and power. We will no longer exercise spiritual government by fleshly means. We will rise and will lift up a standard of righteousness that will destroy the satanic forces that march against us in the name of Jesus.

FALSE IMPRISONMENT

"Plaintiff is entitled to recover damages for what the party wrongfully did."

There are a countless number of pastors that have a secret prison in the church.

They canvas the pulpit like it's a place of victory, but behind the scenes, they are shackled by the scandalous leadership that was put in place to protect them.

The enemy has strategically used the pulpit against the men and women of God to cast them into a spiritual prison. What is meant by this dialogue of *false imprisonment* when we're called by God to *"set the captives free?"*

The spiraling effect of disrespect to the authority of the pastor have opened satanic doors to the enemy. The people of God have been sold a psychological mindset that the pastor doesn't have the right nor authority to tell them what to do. This mindset has perpetrated a spiritual attack so much so that the pastor is unable to effectively lead the people of God.

This creates a rift in the governmental kingdom and causes the oil that flows from the head down unto the people to dry up. The hands of the leader have become so restricted and tied that they are rendered impotent and ineffective to carry out their divine purpose for the church.

The first way the imprisonment of the leader comes from having a negative mindset. If our heart and mind is not stayed upon the Lord, we can become easily enticed to assume the negativity of the people and assist the enemy in opening prison doors to our ministry. When we experience ministry setbacks and disappointments, it tends to affect how the leader preaches, serves, and leads the people.

Our adversity must not be given authority over the Spirit or else it will cause us to go into the inner prison of our mind and feel a since of defeat and despair. When this happens, we block the moving of the Holy Spirit and imprison our own destiny because we find it difficult to believe that God told us we would be blessed and sent to the nations.

We thought *"going to the nations"* meant an instant propelling to greatness, but instead it was a prison sentence to be put in a place of trials and testing. If you don't fully comprehend the *"length, height, depth, and breath of the Lord,"* you can easily violate your calling. The imprisonment of your mind will shift you into a realm of misconception and misunderstanding causing you to blame the Lord for your spiritual imbalance.

Being self-imprisoned is like taking drugs that you know will harm you. You must fight the *"good fight of faith."* Every pastor must not allow their mind to go away from the principles of the Word because the damage could be irreversible if you allow yourself to wear handcuffs and chains to the pulpit each Sunday.

Routinely, you come out of your mental or psychological prison long enough to preach a good word, after the benediction, you put yourself back in prison like it's a normal function. The enemy has secretly stolen your desire to be "free."

For the first time, you sense that your heart is not in it, but you don't want the people to feel as if you don't care. That's truly not the reason you have taken on a cold shoulder or somber attitude. You're behind bars crying out for help in your mind, but your mouth will not let you say it.

Pride, guilt, and shame will not allow the men and women of God to admit that someone needs to pray them out of a spiritual prison. Walking into the church doors on Sunday morning is like going to the mortuary. You were all excited about life until you pulled up on the church grounds.

There was a spirit of oppression waiting for you to arrive and escort you into the pastor study. Because your resistance and discernment are already low, you invited the spirit in without taking authority over it. The enemy begin to cause you to do a survey of the Sunday morning attendance and the results were feed back to you in discouragement.

Again, the enemy has succeeded in keeping you locked up in the mind and now you have closed your spirit man to the enthusiasm of serving the people of God. Your function and responsibility has been clouded by a preconceived notion that you won't have to preach as hard today because the crowd didn't show up.

You picked a Scripture just to get you through the service, but your level of anointing didn't push you as far because the love for the people had been distorted by numbers. You begin to wonder if all your sweating and energy you use while delivering the Word on Sunday morning has any impact on the people, because they seem to just sit there and watch you like they're looking at a television commercial.

There are signs that you're a prisoner to the distraction, but still you have not utilized the spiritual resources available to you. The spirit of oppression is still in your seat and has given you a false sense of security to start thinking negatively about the people of God. This has strategically played a role in keeping you bound to your chains.

You feel the people should be responding to you as the leader, but the spirit that came in with you is the real culprit. Until the men and women of God get the concept that it's not about the people controlling the service, but a spirit, there will be a sense of disrespect and a feeling of unappreciative attitude that will fortify itself against your ability to carry out the assignment.

There must be an awareness of spiritual insight to what type of atmosphere you are ministering in. It would be easy to assume that something is wrong with you, but what you're feeling is the spirit of false imprisonment, which is not only redirecting your thoughts, but also controlling how you preach.

The chains must be broken off the men and women of God in order for the flow of the spirit to come forth. Remember David danced when the Ark of the Covenant was returned from the house of Obededom the Gittite?

While there for only three months, David realized that Obededom house was being blessed. David was so exacerbated about the fact that the presence of the Lord was blessing the house of Obededom and everything that was his, that he purposed to bring the Ark of the Covenant back to the City of David.

When he saw that the glory of the Lord, through the Ark of the Covenant was coming back, *"He made sacrifice and danced before the LORD with all his might." He knew that Israel had no chance of being free or victorious over their enemies without the power and glory of God being in the house."*

Instead of us as leaders given in to what we see as hopelessness, defeat, despair and rejection, we have to break out of our prison by restoring the praise in the house of the Lord. The enemy will not release you unless you're willing to fight back. In order to get your oil back, you have got to start a heavenly invasion against the enemy.

We must refuse to surrender our lives over to the will of the enemy. There has to be a defined purpose and fight left inside of you with a willingness to comprehend the full magnitude of God's purpose in your life.

A NATION WILL NOT BE BIRTHED IF YOU DON'T OVERCOME THE FALSEHOOD OF THE ENEMY.

The Scripture reminds us that, "*The right hand of the LORD is exalted: the right hand of the LORD doeth valiantly. I shall not die, but live, and declare the works of the LORD.*" (Psalm 118:17)

Through the grace of God, you can and must overcome the inner shame and turmoil of the enemy. Just because you're a leader doesn't exempt you from attack. Don't allow the attack to place you in a prison of denial and self- incrimination. Your chains are heavy, but you must not depend your strength, but on the Lord's. The satanic forces are out to stop your influence. Stay out of the realm of opening your feelings to the idea that you're not qualified or inadequate to serve the people of God.

In every prison, there is medical dispensary. In your case, the medicine that's needed is a recharge of the Holy Spirits presence in your life. When you lift your hands up on Sunday morning, the enemy will try to remind you that your seat of authority is none existent.

When you start thinking in retrospect where the Lord has brought you from, then all of a sudden you begin to realize that you were never in a physical prison, but spiritual. Your reaction to the enemy's attacks will determine whether or not if you can break free.

When things are not as they seem, it can be an illusion that has blinded your thinking, feelings, and emotions. If you don't believe that you're free then the spirit of the enemy will continue to be strengthen against you. The anguish of continual bondage will remain in your life. When you acknowledge your imprisonment, and cry out to the Lord for help, **HE WILL COME TO YOUR RESCUE!**

In Acts chapter 16, Paul and Silas prayed while in prison, not out of fear, but in **FAITH.** They believed beyond their circumstance that the Lord could bring them out. The bible says not only did they pray, but they sang praises unto the Lord.

This reaction to their prison created a cataclysmic event that caused the prison experience to be suddenly interrupted. There was a jail break at midnight because the men of God saw the need to utilize the heavenly weapons made available to them.

They exercised their kingdom right to pray and praise which resulted in an uncompromised release from the enemy's bondage. The earth shook, the very foundation of the prison was moved, prison doors came off their hinges, chains fell off, and when the jail house guards came out their sleep they were scared because the prison was not like they left it. They were ready to take their own lives out of fear.

Men, and Women of God, **YOUR DAYS OF FALSE IMPRISIONMENT ARE OVER!!!!** God is about to bring a sudden and miraculous miracle to your house. You will not remain in bondage.   The Lord has called you to **VICTORY!!!**

Not only will you experience a natural manifestation of a Divine intervention from the Lord, but a spiritual renewal of power and boldness to stand up to your enemies and remind them that you have the authority to overcome and stand in victory.

Reclaim your divine rights and heavenly assignment. Don't expect the people to do it for you, go before the Lord with prayer and singing and watch for your suddenly moment. "It's getting ready to happen." What you didn't realize in the false imprisonment was the fact that God is still in control.

If we listen to the Holy Spirit, He will guide us to the victory. Through this stage of your life as a pastor and/or leader, you could only see the bad when in fact, God meant it for good. You had to experience what it really means to be a true servant of the Lord and to further understand the spiritual battle that is against the people of God.

We all know that if the enemy can defeat the under-shepherd he can scatter the flock. **BREAK OUT** men and women of God. Recover your strength to serve. Stand on the authority of the word of God.

"If the Son therefore shall make you free, ye shall be free indeed." (John 8:36)

Now that you've finally realized that the imprisonment was under false pretenses, there is retribution owed for the time that was taken from you as men and women of God.

The Lord says in Deuteronomy 28:7-8, *"The LORD shall cause thine enemies that rise up against thee to be smitten before thy face: they shall come out against the one way, and flee before thee seven ways. The LORD shall command the blessing upon thee in thy storehouses, and in all that thou settest thine hand unto: and he shall bless thee in the land which the LORD thy God giveth thee."*

How do you know that you have been freed from your false imprisonment? When you can drive up on the church grounds, walk in the house of the Lord, stand before any number of people whether large or small, and look out over the congregation and declare

"I was glad when they said unto me, let us go into the house of the LORD." (Psalm 122:1)

At that moment, you come to understand that it's not about you, but the honored privilege it is to be a servant of the **MOST HIGH GOD**. We cast down our chains of oppression, despair, depression, discouragement, hurt, and rejection. We take off the spirit of heaviness and put on the garment of praise. We remove ashes for beauty. There is a heavenly adjustment to our heart, mind, and thoughts.

The spiritual system has been rebooted and we're ready to take the fight to the enemy. He almost destroyed our very existence because we had lost our zeal and purpose. There could have been another church closure because of our blindness to the enemy's attack. The plan was discovered, and the plot to bind us up was defeated. We lift our hands in total praise and there are no chains attached.

We breathe in our new-found dimension of release. The joy of the Lord has been restored to servants of the Lord. Now watch our kingdom advancement. The enemy thought he had us, but we got away. All glory and praise be unto our Lord and Savior, Jesus Christ. Rise up and take your place men and women of God.

There is no more false imprisonment. Repayment for what was lost has been doubled. The glory of the Lord has returned unto our house.

The Pastors & Leaders Spiritual Assessment

The purposes of this assessment is for you the pastor or leader to assess your spiritual awareness of bondages and false imprisonment in your life.

You must not play the enemies game and allow yourself to be injected with this falsehood. Your role is too vital in the kingdom and the responsibility is too great. We must at all cost protect the integrity of the pulpit and hold with true accountability the importance of the Gospel of Jesus Christ. Men and Women of God are silently crying, but it's time for us to shout with a loud voice unto the Lord.

Answer the assessment questions below to see where you might need the Lord to help you as a servant. Every leader must see themselves in order to be free of the things that the enemy may have snuck into our lives unawares.

1.   Do you become discouraged when the people don't celebrate you as a leader?

2.   Are you easily offended when there seem to be no response from your preaching?

3.   Do you find yourself counting the number of people that show up on Sunday morning?

4.   Is your energy of preaching less when you minister to a smaller crowd of people?

5. Do you constantly talk about what the people should be doing for their leader?

6. Are you seemingly always around your members throughout the week?

7. Is the majority of your time spent having activities for your church members rather than for your own family?

8. Are you easily offended from the pulpit when the people don't show up?

9. Can you accept that you will not win everyone in your ministry?

10. Do you fuss at your people from the pulpit about every little thing?

11.   Is your message centered more on fussing at the people or preaching the gospel?

12.   Do find yourself hanging around the people after church every service. You don't leave until everyone has left.

After you have honestly engaged each question, ask the Holy Spirit to show you what you have not recognized about your behavioral patterns as a leader. I would like to suggest asking these few questions as a starting point:

1) What should you change in dealing with the church and the people?

2) Is my approach a reflection of my own insecurities and bondages?

3) What bondages or actions of false imprisonment I may be displaying?

4) Did I allow satanic influences to interfere with my motives?

5)   What do I need to do in order to break chains and open prison doors in my life?

Now you have to begin to the process of repentance, forgiveness, healing, and restoration. When we as leaders take ownership of what the Lord has assigned to our lives, the *"Lord is faithful and just to forgive us and to cleanse us from all unrighteousness."* (I John 1:8-9)

Our testimony of victory and deliverance is an ultimate conquest over satanic forces that came out to stop the servants of the Lord.

We have to ensure that our prison break from the enemies' falsehood and bondages are intentional and evident. **OUR FREEDOM AS LEADERS IS NECESSARY,** so that we can be a Godly example before the people of God.

Ministry & Booking Info

Address: P.O. Box 25191 Fayetteville, NC 28314

Email: bishopfuller@yahoo.com